HISTORY & GEOGRAPHY 503
A TIME OF TESTING

Author:
Theresa Buskey, J.D.

Editor:
Alan Christopherson, M.S.

Media Credits:
Page 3: © Anthony Totah ,Hemera,Thinkstock; **5, 39:** © Steven Wynn, iStock, Thinkstock; **8:** © Dynamic Graphics 2007, liquidlibrary, Thinkstock; **9:** © alancrosthwaite, iStock, Thinkstock; **11:** © Dorling Kindersley, Thinkstock; **12:** © Christopher Paquette, iStock,Thinkstock; **14:** © Christoffer Wilhelm Eckersberg, Randers Art Museum; **15:** © Gary Tognoni, iStock,Thinkstock; **16:** © Photos.com, Thinkstock; **21:** © AdamParent , iStock, Thinkstock; **23:** © Jean,Marc labal, iStock, Thinkstock; **25:** J. Carl Burke, Jr., United States Library of Congress; **26:** © George Munger, The White House Historical Association; © Zack Frank, iStock, Thinkstock; **27:** © Courtesy of the Navy Art Collection, Washington, D.C.; **28:** © ClaudineVM, iStock, Thinsktock; **29:** © akova, iStock, Thinkstock; © Jean Hyacinthe de Laclotte, New Orleans Museum of Art; **30:** © Eugene Gurevich, Hemera, Thinkstock; **31:** © Mark Stephenson, iStock, Thinkstock; **37:** © David Biagi , iStock, Thinkstock; **40, 46:** © Denis Kozlenko, iStock, Thinkstock; © vaeenma, iStock, Thinkstock; **41:** © Sharon Day, iStock, Thinkstock; **44:** © Sourabh Jain, iStock, Thinkstock; **48:** © alexeys, iStock, Thinkstock; **49:** © mechanerfer, iStock, Thinkstock; **50:** © Aneese, iStock, Thinkstock.

All maps in this book © Map Resources, unless otherwise stated.

Alpha Omega
PUBLICATIONS

804 N. 2nd Ave. E.
Rock Rapids, IA 51246-1759

A TIME OF TESTING

France was at war with Britain and other countries for many of the years between 1792 and 1815. These wars proved to be a large headache for the United States. America tried to stay neutral. However, the British and the French wanted to stop the Americans from trading with their enemy. Both sides stopped American ships that were trying to bring goods to one side or the other for sale. They often seized the cargo and took it for their own nation!

However, the British were the worst. They took American citizens! The British navy needed seamen for the war and they often took them off any American ships they stopped. This stealing of people angered America so much that we went to war again with Britain in 1812.

This was a time of testing for the young United States. The problems leading up the war tested the nation as much as the war itself. The states and people had to keep working together, obeying the government during some hard times. They had to rebuild afterward. Then, the country had to face the issue of slavery which was already threatening to divide the north from the south.

Objectives

Read these objectives. The objectives tell you what you will be able to do when you have successfully completed this LIFEPAC. Each section will list according to the numbers below what objectives will be met in that section. When you have finished this LIFEPAC, you should be able to:

1. Describe the beliefs and actions of Thomas Jefferson as president.
2. Describe the continuing battles between the United States and the Native Americans.
3. Explain why the war in Europe caused problems for the United States and how Jefferson tried to solve those problems.
4. List the reasons why the U.S. went to war with Britain in 1812.
5. Describe the major battles and name the important heroes of the War of 1812.
6. Describe the way the War of 1812 ended and its results.
7. Describe the changes and important events of the years after the War of 1812.
8. Describe the important changes in transportation in America in the early 1800s.

1. JEFFERSON

Thomas Jefferson became president in 1801 with very strong ideas about what the president should and should not do. He found, however, that the needs of the job were bigger than his ideas. He bought a huge chunk of land to add to the country, even though he believed he should not. He set the navy into battle with pirates, sent out a famous scientific expedition, and even stopped all American trade. He acted much stronger as president than his own ideas should have permitted. He also was unable to stop the growing problems with Britain. Shortly after he left office, America declared war on Britain.

While Jefferson was president, Americans continued to move onto the frontier. The land prices were low, but the work was hard. People on the frontier lived in log cabins that they built with their own hands, and there were few stores from which to buy things. Yet, the nation grew as more people moved west and more states were added to the Union.

Objectives

Review these objectives. When you have completed this section, you should be able to:

1. Describe the beliefs and actions of Thomas Jefferson as president.
2. Describe the continuing battles between the United States and the Native Americans.
3. Explain why the war in Europe caused problems for the United States and how Jefferson tried to solve those problems.
4. List the reasons why the U.S. went to war with Britain in 1812.

Vocabulary

Study these new words. Learning the meanings of these words is a good study habit and will improve your understanding of this LIFEPAC.

desert (di zėrt′). To go away and leave a person or place, especially one that should not be left; forsake.

dictator (dik′ tā tər). A person who rules, using complete authority.

expedition (ek′ spə dish′ ən). A journey for a special purpose, such as exploration or scientific study.

ransom (ran′ səm). The price paid or demanded before a captive is set free.

sapling (sap′ ling). A young tree.

shingle (shing′ gəl). A thin piece of wood or other material, used to cover roofs and walls; shingles are laid in overlapping rows with the thicker end showing.

subdue (səb dü′). To overcome by force; conquer.

Note: *All vocabulary words in this LIFEPAC appear in* **boldface** *print the first time they are used. If you are not sure of the meaning when you are reading, study the definitions given.*

Pronunciation Key: hat, āge, cãre, fär; let, ēqual, tėrm; it, īce; hot, ōpen, ôrder; oil; out; cup, pu̇t, rüle; child; long; thin; /ᵺH/ for then; /zh/ for measure; /u/ or /ə/ represents /a/ in about, /e/ in taken, /i/ in pencil, /o/ in lemon, and /u/ in circus.

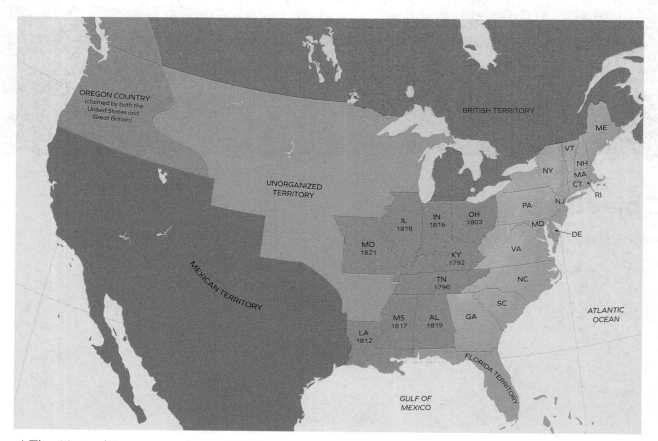

| The United States in about 1830

Land and Pirates

Jefferson. Our third president, Thomas Jefferson, was a very brilliant man. He read all kinds of books. He was very interested in science. He had traveled around Europe when he replaced Benjamin Franklin as our representative in France. He loved to try new ideas and invent useful items for his home, like swiveling chairs. He had been active in the government since his home state of Virginia had been a British colony. He had a talent for writing that he used to write the Declaration of Independence.

Jefferson also had some strong ideas about what the United States should be and how it should be run. He wanted his country to be a nation of farmers, not factories. He wanted a small, weak national government. He also firmly believed that the common people should rule themselves. Remember, the idea in Europe was that the nobles ruled and the people obeyed. Many of the leaders in America still kept parts of that idea. They distrusted ordinary people and wanted only people with wealth and power to rule. Thomas Jefferson was one of the people who changed this in America. He worked to give more people the right to vote and end things that limited their freedom, like government churches. Soon, the idea that the people ruled would be accepted all over in the United States. However, Jefferson's other ideas about a weak federal government and a nation of farmers were not as successful.

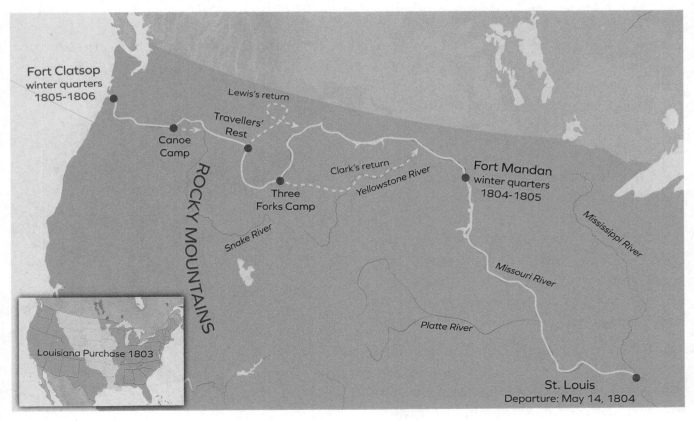

| The Lewis and Clark Expedition / The Louisiana Purchase

Thomas Jefferson tried to keep to his ideas at first. He ran the government as cheaply as he could. He ended the tax on whiskey. He paid off as much of the government's debts as he could. He also did not spend much money on the navy and the army. As a result, the country was not ready to defend itself when the warring nations in Europe began taking American ships, goods, and people.

Louisiana Purchase. The land east of the Mississippi River belonged to America. Before the Revolution, the land west of the Mississippi (up to the Rocky Mountains) had belonged to Spain. However, Spain returned it to France in about 1800. In 1803, France offered to sell all of this land, called Louisiana, to the United States for $15 million!

Thomas Jefferson did not know what to do! The Constitution did not say anything about buying more territory. If he followed his own ideas about the Constitution and a weak federal government, he would have to refuse. However, the land was very valuable and that was a good price for it (about 3¢ an acre). The purchase would almost double the size of the country. It would also give America complete control of the Mississippi River which was needed as a highway into the territories west of the Appalachians. Jefferson realized he could not pass this up. He agreed to buy the land. We call this land the *Louisiana Purchase*.

Lewis and Clark. No one knew what was in the vast, empty land America had just bought. One writer told tales of a salt mountain one hundred and eighty miles long and forty-five miles wide. Other people were concerned that dinosaurs might live there after some of their bones were found. Jefferson, the scientist, decided to find out.

Jefferson sent a special expedition out to explore the Louisiana Purchase. Jefferson's secretary, a soldier named Meriwether Lewis, was one of the leaders. The other was William Clark, a former soldier and the younger brother of the Revolutionary hero George Rogers Clark. Their trip was called the *Lewis and Clark Expedition*.

The Lewis and Clark Expedition left St. Louis, Missouri, a frontier town, in May of 1804. They traveled up the Missouri River toward the Rocky Mountains. All along the way they collected plants and took careful notes. They took notes on the animals, the climate, the weather, the Indians, and many other things. They stopped for the winter in North Dakota.

There they met a Shoshone Indian woman named Sacagawea. She was a big help to them. She showed the expedition a way over the Rocky Mountains in the spring, carrying

| Lewis and Clark

her baby on her back as she went. They met her brother on the trip. He traded with the Americans for food and other supplies they needed. The expedition crossed all the way over the Rocky Mountains. It traveled down the Columbia River in Oregon and reached the Pacific Ocean. These were the very first Americans ever to cross the continent by land.

They spent the winter by the ocean and started back in the spring. They finally got back to St. Louis in September of 1806. They had traveled about 8,000 miles by canoe, horseback, and foot. They brought back thousands of samples and notes. There was so much information that it took until 1815 to put it together and publish it (and that book did not include everything). The expedition told Americans a great deal about their new land and gave the United States a claim to Oregon.

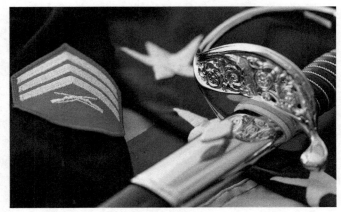

| The U.S. Marines first major action was in Tripoli.

Barbary Coast. The north coast of Africa, called the Barbary Coast, was the home of many pirates in 1800. These people would capture trading ships that sailed into the Mediterranean Sea, holding the ships and sailors for **ransom**. The only way a nation could protect its ships was to pay huge bribes to the pirates every year. When Jefferson was president, the U.S. was paying one of these nations, Tripoli, $2 million a year (which was a lot of money at the time). In 1801, the Pasha (ruler) of Tripoli decided he wanted more and began attacking American ships.

By that time, Jefferson had enough. He ordered the small American navy to attack Tripoli. The navy fought very well, earning the respect of not only the pirates but also European nations. Finally, the Pasha agreed to a much smaller payment. After even more fighting later, the payments were stopped altogether. The officers and sailors in the U.S. Navy learned a great deal in this small war that would help them in 1812 when America declared war on Britain.

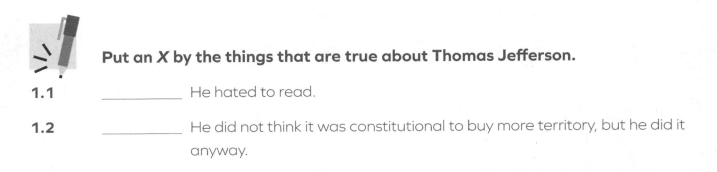

Put an _X_ by the things that are true about Thomas Jefferson.

1.1 _____ He hated to read.

1.2 _____ He did not think it was constitutional to buy more territory, but he did it anyway.

1.3 _____ He wanted the rich and powerful to rule.

1.4 _____ He wanted a nation of farmers.

1.5 _____ He ran the government as cheaply as possible.

1.6 _____ He kept the U.S. Navy strong.

1.7 _____ He wanted a weak national government.

1.8 _____ He put the federal government deeper in debt.

1.9 _____ He liked to invent useful things.

Complete these sentences.

1.10 The United States bought the land west of the Mississippi River, called the
_____ Purchase, from France for
_____ dollars.

1.11 The leaders of the scientific expedition sent to explore America's new land were
_____ and _____ .
This expedition explored the _____ River in Oregon and
reached the _____ Ocean over land.

1.12 A Shoshone Indian woman named _____ helped the
_____ Expedition to find a way across the
Rocky Mountains.

1.13 Thomas Jefferson sent the American navy to attack the pirate nation of
_____ on the north coast of Africa.

1.14 Pirates on the Barbary Coast would capture ships and sailors to hold for
_____ .

Growing Bigger

Frontier. Nations have a character in the same way that people do. The character of the United States had a lot to do with the frontier. For many, many years, the U.S. always had a frontier, a place of wilderness where anyone could go, buy land, and start a new life. It was usually a hard life, and it built strong people. Americans, as a result, became very strong, independent, freedom loving people. This only changed in this last 100 years.

Many people moved to the frontier every year in America. New states were added all the time until about 1900. Vermont was the very first state to join the Union in 1791. Kentucky joined in 1792 and Tennessee just a few years later. By the beginning of 1820, the United States had twenty-two states. The country would continue to add states until it had fifty of them by 1959.

The main reason people moved west was to have their own land and make a better life for themselves. The good farmland in the east usually belonged to someone already. For as little as $80 to start and three more $80 payments later, a man could have a 320-acre farm on the frontier in 1800. This was a great opportunity, and Americans just kept moving out to do it.

The people who dared to try life on the frontier were called *pioneers*. The word is used for people who are the first at something. A 1901 American history book described a pioneer's home like this:

> Once [on the frontier], the "mover," the "newcomer," would [move onto] his land, cut down a few small trees, and make a half faced camp. This was a shed with three sides of logs and the fourth side open. When it rained, the open side was closed by hanging up deerskins.
>
> In the half-faced camp the settler lived till his log cabin was finished. If he made his home in a place where there were other settlers, they would all come and help build the cabin. These frontier homes rarely had more than one window and one door. As glass was scarce and costly, the window frame was often covered with greased paper, which let in the light but could not be seen through.
>
> The builder [of a log cabin] would begin by cutting down trees and chopping them into logs about fourteen feet long and notching the end halfway through. When enough had been cut he would place four on the ground in the shape of a square, taking care to leave an open space in one side for a doorway, and another at one end for a

| Log cabin

huge fireplace. On top of these he would put a second set of logs, and then a third and a fourth, and so on till the walls were as high as he wished them to be.

For the roof he used log rafters, placed **saplings** across them, and on the saplings laid marsh grass or straw, or bark of trees like **shingles**, or shingles themselves if he had time to make them. Between the walls of logs of course would be chinks or open spaces, because tree trunks, being of different shapes, would not everywhere touch each other. These chinks were filled with [wood] chips covered with mud or clay. Outside the great fireplace was the chimney, made either of stones, or of branches of trees covered with clay on the inside to keep them from taking fire. Stoves and ranges were unknown.

The tables and chairs were made by the settler. His brooms and brushes were of corn husks, and many of his utensils were cut out of tree trunks. If the man was industrious, he would of course get a better house in time. But in pioneer days a large part of the settlers lived and died in log cabins. (McMaster, John Bach. *A Primary History of the United States.* American Book Co. 1901)

Native Americans. Americans began to settle west of the Appalachian Mountains about the time of the Revolution. The Indians there always fought to stop the pioneers. After the war, the British still hoped to regain the land they lost. They deliberately traded with the Indians, giving them guns and ammunition to fight the American settlers. The Native Americans succeeded in stopping two American armies sent to **subdue** them in the Northwest Territory around 1790. However, the Americans did not give up easily.

| Tecumseh

Almost 2,000 Indian warriors gathered in 1794 to fight a new American army near Toledo, Ohio. The Americans were led by General "Mad Anthony" Wayne. He was a hero of the Revolution who had earned his nickname for his daring attacks in that war. The Native American army was crushed in the Battle of Fallen Timbers, which lasted less than an hour.

About ten years later, a very remarkable Indian chief from the Shawnee people tried again. His name was Tecumseh, and he planned very carefully. He traveled all along the Mississippi River, talking to the tribes that lived there. He convinced them that the only chance they had was to work together to defeat the Americans. Many of the tribes joined an alliance called the Tecumseh Confederacy.

While Tecumseh was organizing the Confederacy in the south, his brother, a Shawnee religious leader, was left in charge of the Confederacy in the north. The brother, called the Prophet, refused to obey a treaty his tribe had signed to move out of some of their land. The governor of the Indiana Territory, William Henry Harrison, led out the militia to remove them in 1811. The Prophet attacked first at the Battle of Tippecanoe. The Indians were defeated and the Confederacy was badly hurt.

Tecumseh convinced some of the tribes to join the British in its new war with America in 1812. They helped with many of the early victories for the British in the Northwest Territory. However, Tecumseh was killed in battle in 1813 and that ended the Confederacy.

Name the person, battle, or item.

1.15 _____ Battle against the Shawnee Prophet in Indiana (1811) _____ and the name of the territorial governor who led the militia

1.16 _____ Number of U.S. states at the beginning of 1820

1.17 _____ How much money <u>total</u> a man had to pay for a frontier farm of 320 acres in 1800

1.18 _____ Name for people who moved to the frontier

1.19 _____ Type of house most frontier settlers lived in

1.20 _____ Battle between the Indians and Americans in Ohio, _____ 1794 and the Revolutionary War hero who led the U.S. Army

1.21 _____ Shawnee chief who formed an Indian Confederacy in the early 1800s

1.22 _____ First state added to the Union after the original thirteen

1.23 _____ Nation that gave guns and ammunition to the Indians in the Northwest Territory after the Revolution

British Problems

Impressment. Life in the British navy was very difficult. Sailors had bad food, filthy places to sleep, no freedom, and they were beaten anytime they broke the ship's rules. As a result, few people wanted to work as sailors on the ships. Many of the sailors were men seized in Britain and forced to work in the navy. Some British sailors would **desert** their ships and go to work on American ships. They were treated much better there. Many of these men even became U.S. citizens.

During the long war with France, Britain desperately needed men for its navy. They were stopping U.S. ships to make sure they were not trading with France. They began to search those ships for British sailors who had escaped. However, they needed men so badly that they were not at all careful about who they took.

A British warship would stop an American merchant ship sailing on the ocean. The American ship was usually unarmed while the British ship had cannons. The Americans had no choice but to let the British come aboard.

A British officer would check the cargo and take it if he thought it might be headed for France.

| British warship attacking the *U.S.S. Chesapeake*

He would then line up all the sailors on the deck. He would pick out the men he wanted, claim they were British, and take them away into a life that was like slavery. This was called "impressment" because the men were "pressed" (forced) into service in the British navy.

Naturally, this made Americans very angry to have their fellow citizens treated this way, but the American navy was too small to stop it. The British had the largest navy in the world at that time. The British did not care what the Americans thought. They even attacked an American warship called the *U.S.S. Chesapeake*, killed several men, and took four sailors off it in 1807.

Embargo. Thomas Jefferson wanted to stop the impressments and the taking of American cargoes by both sides in Europe. He was not willing to raise taxes and build a navy to defend American trade, so he decided to <u>stop</u> <u>all</u> American trade. He believed that would hurt Britain and France. They would not be able to sell their tea, tools, and cloth in America. They also could not buy food and supplies from us. Jefferson hoped they would lose enough money that they would agree to stop taking cargoes and men.

This was called an *embargo*. The Embargo Act of 1807 forbade any American goods to be sent out in any ships. It was not a good idea. All it did was hurt Americans. People who sailed the ships lost their jobs. People who loaded and unloaded them lost theirs. Shipbuilders had no work. Farmers could not sell their cash crops like wheat, cotton, and tobacco in Europe. The people of America were losing money, while it did not really bother Britain or France. They both refused to stop taking Americans ships or men.

People in America hated the embargo. They called it the "o-grab-me" ("embargo" spelled backwards). They became very angry with Thomas Jefferson. Finally, he repealed (took back) the Embargo Act in 1809.

| American cargo was seized

War Hawks. Americans were now very angry with Britain. The British were taking U.S. cargoes, taking men off our ships, supplying the Indians with guns, and still would not give up their forts in the Northwest Territory. Some of the men elected to Congress around this time began to demand war for these four reasons. They were called the *War Hawks*.

The War Hawks came mainly from the new states in the west and south. These were young men who had not fought in the Revolutionary War. They did not remember the suffering of the last war. The War Hawks foolishly wanted to capture Canada. They wanted to add it to the United States. They thought that would be easy to do because Britain was busy fighting in Europe and could not stop an American invasion. They also wanted to stop the Indian attacks by getting rid of the British who were giving them guns.

Other parts of the country did not want war. New England needed its trade with Britain to make money. Many people there did not want war with Britain. In fact, many of them wanted to help Britain defeat the French **dictator**, Napoleon, who had conquered all of Europe.

James Madison, the father of the Constitution, became our fourth president in 1809. He did not know what to do. He tried several different ideas to get the Europeans to respect American ships. Nothing worked. Finally, he gave in to the arguments of the War Hawks and asked Congress to declare war on Britain. They did so in 1812. We call this war the *War of 1812*. It is also called the *Second War for Independence*, because we fought to force Britain to respect our rights as a free and equal country.

| Napoleon Bonaparte

Answer these questions.

1.24 What was the nickname given to the young men elected to Congress who wanted war?

_____

1.25 How did Thomas Jefferson try to stop the taking of American cargo and men?

_____

1.26 Who was our fourth president? _____

1.27 What was it called when the British took men off American ships?

_____

1.28 What were the four reasons why the U.S. went to war with Britain?

_____

_____

1.29 What did people who hated the embargo call it? _____

1.30 What part of the country did not want war with Britain? _____

1.31 What are the two names for the second war America had with Britain?

_____

_____

1.32 What land did the War Hawks hope to capture? _____

1.33 What U.S. warship was attacked by the British and had four sailors taken?

_____

Review the material in this section to prepare for the Self Test. The Self Test will check your understanding of this section. Any items you miss on this test will show you what areas you will need to restudy in order to prepare for the unit test.

SELF TEST 1

Match these people. Some answers will be used more than once (each answer, 3 points).

1.01 _____ Fourth U.S. president

1.02 _____ Kept taxes too low to build a large navy

1.03 _____ Jefferson's secretary, expedition leader in Louisiana

1.04 _____ Shoshone woman, aided expedition exploring Louisiana

1.05 _____ Asked Congress to declare war on Britain

1.06 _____ Indiana territorial governor, defeated the Indians at Tippecanoe

1.07 _____ Shawnee chief, formed an Indian Confederacy

1.08 _____ Expedition leader in Louisiana, soldier and brother of a Revolutionary war hero

1.09 _____ Revolutionary war hero, defeated the Indians at Fallen Timbers

1.010 _____ Bought Louisiana for the U.S.

a. Thomas Jefferson

b. James Madison

c. William Clark

d. Meriwether Lewis

e. Tecumseh

f. Sacagawea

g. "Mad Anthony" Wayne

h. William Henry Harrison

Fill in the blanks to finish these sentences (each answer, 4 points).

1.011 The group sent out to explore Louisiana by Thomas Jefferson was called the

_____ Expedition.

1.012 Jefferson sent the American navy to attack the pirates on the

_____ Coast in 1801.

1.013 People who moved to the frontier were called _____ .

1.014 Americans were angry because the _____ were

supplying the Indians in the Northwest Territory with guns.

1.015 Thomas Jefferson tried to get the Europeans to respect American ships by stopping

all U.S. trade with an _____ in 1807.

1.016 The young Congressmen who wanted war were called

_____ .

1.017 America's second war with Britain was called the

_____ .

1.018 Most people who moved to the frontier lived in _____ .

1.019 America bought all of the land west of the Mississippi River, called the

_____ , from France in 1803 for $15 million.

1.020 British officers took men off American ships, a practice called

_____ .

Write _true_ or _false_ in the blank (each answer, 3 points).

1.021 _____ The Rocky Mountain Expedition gave America a claim to Oregon.

1.022 _____ Jefferson believed America should be ruled by the common people.

1.023 _____ Americans could pay $320 in four payments to buy a 320 acre frontier
farm in 1800.

1.024 _____ The Pasha of Tripoli was an American ally.

1.025 _____ The frontier helped make Americans strong, independent, and freedom
loving.

1.026 _____ Life was fair and easy in the British navy.

1.027 _____ The American warship, *U.S.S. Chesapeake*, attacked a British warship to take back a cargo removed from an American ship in 1807.

1.028 _____ New England wanted war with Britain.

1.029 _____ The Congressmen who wanted war hoped to add Canada to the United States.

1.030 _____ America's second war with Britain is sometimes called the Second War for Independence.

Teacher check:

Score _____

Initials _____

Date _____

80 / 100

2. WAR OF 1812

Americans had been avoiding another war with Britain since George Washington's second term. He had kept America neutral when France and Britain began their war. Now, American pride had been pushed too far. The constant loss of American ships, cargoes, and men was too much. Also, the British would not leave the Northwest Territory. So, under President Madison, the War of 1812 began.

America was not well prepared for war. They assumed that Britain would be busy in Europe and that they could just take Canada. However, the former Frenchmen in Canada and the Tories who had fled there after the American Revolution fought bravely for their homeland. Then the war ended in Europe, and Britain turned all of its might on America.

The U.S. suffered some humiliating defeats, including having Washington, D.C. burned. The British demanded all sorts of things before they would make peace. However, the Americans regrouped and won several key battles. At last, the British agreed to end the war and respect America's lands. Our Second War for Independence won us respect as an equal nation.

Objectives

Review these objectives. When you have completed this section, you should be able to:

2. Describe the continuing battles between the United States and the Native Americans.
4. List the reasons why the U.S. went to war with Britain in 1812.
5. Describe the major battles and name the important heroes of the War of 1812.
6. Describe the way the War of 1812 ended and its results.

Vocabulary

Study these new words. Learning the meanings of these words is a good study habit and will improve your understanding of this LIFEPAC.

blockade (blo kād'). The blocking of a place by an army or navy to control who or what goes into or out of it.

bombard (bom bärd'). To attack with bombs or heavy fire from big guns.

foreign (fôr' ən). Coming from outside one's own country.

gut (gut). To destroy the inside of something.

honorable (on' ər ə bəl). Having or showing a sense of what is right and proper; honest; upright.

orderly (ôr' dər lē). A soldier who attends a superior officer to carry orders.

priceless (prīs' lis). Very valuable.

Pronunciation Key: h**a**t, **ā**ge, c**ã**re, f**ä**r; l**e**t, **ē**qual, t**ė**rm; **i**t, **ī**ce; h**o**t, **ō**pen, **ô**rder; **oi**l; **ou**t; c**u**p, p**u̇**t, r**ü**le; **ch**ild; lo**ng**; **th**in; /ŦH/ for **th**en; /zh/ for mea**s**ure; /u/ or /ə/ represents /a/ in **a**bout, /e/ in tak**e**n, /i/ in penc**i**l, /o/ in lem**o**n, and /u/ in circ**u**s.

War Begins

America was not ready for a war. Jefferson's Democratic-Republicans were in control of Congress. They believed in a weak federal government and low taxes. They had not raised taxes and gathered money to prepare for war, even after they were sure it would happen. The American army had less than 10,000 men in it. The army was especially short of trained officers who knew how to lead a war. The navy had about 20 ships, while the British navy had hundreds. The country would pay for its failure to prepare.

Canada. The very first thing the Americans did after declaring war was to invade Canada. The Canadians defended their homes bravely. Many of the people there were Tories who had left the United States during the Revolution. They did not want to be part of our nation now. The other citizens were the Frenchmen of New France. Britain had been very fair with them, allowing them to keep their religion and customs. They also fought hard against the American invasion.

The Americans had other problems, too. Many of the men in the state militias refused to leave the country. They would not fight in Canada. None of the American armies were successful. Moreover, the American fort at Detroit was taken by the British. The invasion was a total failure.

The American government put William Henry Harrison, the hero of Tippecanoe, in command the next year. He realized he could not retake Detroit while the British could use the Great Lakes to move their men and supplies. He ordered Captain Oliver Perry to get control of the lakes.

Perry built a small fleet on the lakes to do this job. In September of 1813, his fleet met the British ships in the Battle of Lake Erie. It was a fierce fight. Perry's flagship, the ship he commanded the battle from, was destroyed and sunk. Perry got into a rowboat, moved to another American ship and kept fighting. In the end, the British fleet was defeated and captured. Perry sent a wonderful, brief message back to the president, "We have met the enemy and they are ours."

After that victory, the British soldiers left Detroit. William Henry Harrison caught them at the Thames River just inside Canada and defeated them. That allowed the Americans to regain control of all the land near Detroit. However, the Americans were not able to capture Canada.

Navy. While the armies were fighting without much result in Canada, the small American navy was doing great things. The American ships were meeting the British ships in one-on-one battles and winning. The Americans won 13 out of the 16 battles like this during the war.

The most famous American ship of the War of 1812 was the *U.S.S. Constitution.* It was responsible for three American victories at sea. The ship was made of solid oak, a very hard wood. The U.S. sailors claimed that a British cannon ball just bounced off its sides. Because of this, the ship was nicknamed "Old Ironsides." The American people loved the ship so much that they would not allow it to be destroyed when it got old. It was rebuilt several times and is still afloat today. It is also still officially a ship of the United States Navy. It is usually docked in Boston.

| *U.S.S. Constitution*

The British navy was very embarrassed by the American victories. They ordered their ships to sail in pairs to stop them. They also **blockaded** the American coast after the war ended in Europe. This made it difficult for the warships to get supplies and get out to attack the British. It also ruined what was left of America's trade and stopped all tariff money for the government. Without tariff money, the American government could not pay most of its bills. Many people in America were also put out of work when trade was stopped again. Things were bad in America and about to get worse.

The British had a huge army it had been using in Europe. They won that war early in 1814. Now they planned to defeat the Americans in several quick battles, using the soldiers who were no longer needed in Europe. They did not want to retake all of the U.S., just make it give up large parts of its territory. For a time it looked like they might succeed.

Name the person, battle, event, or item.

2.1 _____ The most famous U.S. ship of the War of 1812

2.2 _____ American victory that chased the British off the Great Lakes

2.3 _____ Country the Americans tried to invade

2.4 _____ Important American fort captured by the British in 1812; the Americans got it back the next year

2.5 _____ Man who said, "We have met the enemy and they are ours."

2.6 _____ How many out of sixteen ship-on-ship battles the Americans won

2.7 _____ What the British used to stop all of America's trade and tariff money

2.8 _____ American who won the Battle of the Thames River

2.9 _____ Americans who had moved to Canada during the Revolution

2.10 _____ What Congress should have raised to prepare for war

Dark Days Turn Brighter

The last year of the War of 1812 (1814) was a year that had some very dark days for the Americans. The British won several victories. They were so confident that they made demands for U.S. land before they would make peace. However, the Americans did not give up. They won several important battles of their own. The British realized they could not win without another long war. Britain was sick of war after fighting in Europe for so long, so they finally offered **honorable** terms for peace that the U.S. accepted.

Canada again. The Americans still wanted to take Canada. They invaded it again in 1814. The Americans won a battle at Chippewa and then lost another at Lundy's Lane in July. The Americans took and held Fort Erie in Canada for a few months, but then had to leave. Once again, the Americans were unable to take Canada.

British demands. The large British navy had complete control over the coast of the United States by 1814. They attacked and captured part of the state of Maine. The British were also holding Fort Niagara at Buffalo, New York (they lost it later). Indian allies of the British had made the Northwest Territory very dangerous for settlers and soldiers. Britain, therefore, felt it was winning the war.

| Fort Niagara

The two sides began to meet in 1814 to discuss peace. The British demanded that the U.S. give up part of the Northwest Territory to make a nation for the Indians. The British wanted this nation to block any American invasion of Canada. The British also wanted control of all of the Great Lakes and a big piece of Maine to add to Canada. The American representatives refused to even consider these demands. They trusted their countrymen to fight back and force the British to offer a better peace.

Burning of Washington. The British navy in Chesapeake Bay moved in to attack the American cities there in 1814. In August, they landed an army to attack the capital, Washington, D.C. The Americans had not expected an attack there and were not ready. The small militia force that tried to defend the city was easily beaten and the British army marched into Washington.

They found the city very empty. Most of the citizens had run away. Government papers had been taken away or hidden. President Madison had ridden to the battle and retreated with the army. His wife, Dolley Madison, also fled. However, she did not leave until she had removed many of the valuable things in the president's house.

Dolley Madison had stayed all day while the British were advancing on Washington. She bravely worked to pack important papers and valuables into wagons so they could be moved to safety. She stayed until she could hear the cannons firing! One of the last things she took out was a **priceless** painting of George Washington by Gilbert Stuart. She had it broken out of its frame so it could be moved more easily. But, at last, even she left the endangered city.

| The White House burned by the British

The British burned most of the public buildings in Washington. The president's mansion was completely **gutted**. (It was rebuilt, painted white, and renamed the "White House" after the war.) Fearing an attack by the American army, the British left after they had finished with their destruction. However, the damage to the nation's capital angered the American people, and angry Americans can be dangerous enemies.

Baltimore. The British moved on to attack Baltimore by land and sea. However, the Americans were ready for them this time and they wanted revenge for Washington. The British land army met stiff fighting and was forced to retreat. The British navy **bombarded** Fort McHenry, which protected Baltimore harbor, trying to force it to surrender. The attack continued all night. When it failed, the British withdrew.

| Fort McHenry

One young man watched the battle with great interest. Francis Scott Key, an American, had come aboard a British ship to ask them to release a prisoner. The British made him spend the night there while the battle was raging. He watched anxiously for dawn to see if the American flag was still flying over the fort (that would mean it had not surrendered). He was so delighted to see the Stars and Stripes in the morning that he wrote a poem about it and set it to music. It is the "Star Spangled Banner," our national anthem.

Plattsburgh Bay. The two most important navy battles of the War of 1812 were fought on lakes, not the ocean. The first was the Battle of Lake Erie. The second was the Battle of Plattsburgh Bay on Lake Champlain.

You may remember from the LIFEPAC on the Revolution that Lake Champlain was a water route that could be used to invade New York from Canada. The British general "Gentleman Johnny" Burgoyne had come down that way and been defeated at Saratoga. In 1814 another British army tried it with a small fleet of ships to assist them.

The Americans built a small navy to stop them. The two sides fought a desperate battle at Plattsburgh Bay in September in which many men died. Thomas Macdonough was the American commander. He and his men won a great victory that day. The British retreated, leaving New York alone.

| Macdonough's victory on Lake Champlain

Give the information requested.

2.11 The two important navy battles of the War of 1812:

_____

2.12 The city burned by the British: _____

2.13 American commander who successfully defended Lake Champlain:

_____

2.14 Two battles in Canada in 1814, one an American victory, the other a loss:

_____

2.15 The state that the British wanted to take a piece of: _____

2.16 Man who wrote the "Star Spangled Banner": _____

2.17 Fort that defended Baltimore harbor: _____

2.18 First Lady who saved many of the valuable things in the White House from the British:

_____

2.19 The people the British wanted to have a nation between the U.S. and Canada:

_____

How It Ended

Treaty of Ghent. The Americans and British had been meeting in the city of Ghent in Europe to discuss peace. The British had tried to get a treaty that would give them U.S. land early in 1814. However, later in the year the British heard about the American victories at Baltimore and Plattsburgh Bay. They realized the Americans would not be easily beaten.

They had a choice. They could send more men and fight a long, hard war or they could just quit. Britain had been at war with France for about 20 years. The British people were sick of war. Britain decided to make peace with America.

The two sides signed the Treaty of Ghent in December of 1814, ending the War of 1812. Both sides agreed to stop fighting and return any land that was not theirs. Nothing was said in the treaty about impressment. However, the British had already decided to stop it. The navy did not need men so badly now. Nothing was said about giving guns to the Indians, either. However, the death of Tecumseh had ended the Indian alliance. After the war, the British were not as willing to give guns to the Indians. Thus, some of America's reasons for going to war were solved, even if was not done by the treaty.

| Monument to the Treaty of Ghent

New Orleans. America's biggest victory came after the War of 1812 had ended. The treaty was signed in Europe at the end of 1814. The news did not reach America until late January of 1815. Before it did, the British attacked New Orleans and were soundly defeated.

The British had been planning an attack on New Orleans for several months. Control of the mouth of the Mississippi would allow them to threaten all the cities on the river. They had gathered an army in the West Indies to do the job. However, they had not counted on the American commander, Andrew Jackson.

Andrew Jackson was the son of poor immigrant parents. His father had died before he was born. He lost his mother and both brothers during the Revolutionary War. He had actually joined the militia during the Revolution at the age of thirteen, working as an **orderly**.

| Andrew Jackson

Andrew Jackson was a very proud and hot tempered young man. He was captured by the British in 1781 when he was fourteen. One of the British officers ordered the young man to clean his boots. Jackson refused because he was a prisoner of war, not a servant. The officer became so angry that he attacked Jackson with his sword. Andrew put up his left hand to protect himself. The sword cut him deeply across the hand and forehead. He carried those scars for the rest of his life.

Jackson moved to Tennessee and became a lawyer when he was older. He became rich and built himself a large mansion called the Hermitage on his land near Nashville, Tennessee. He became a leader in politics and the state militia. He was very popular with the men who fought under him. They called him "Old Hickory" because he was so tough. In 1814 he and the Tennessee militia defeated the Creek Indians (who had been attacking settlers) at the Battle of Horseshoe Bend. The U.S. government noticed the victory, made him a general in the regular army, and sent him to defend New Orleans.

Jackson worked quickly to be ready for the British. He captured the Spanish town of Pensacola, Florida. That stopped the British from using it as a base to attack New Orleans. He then moved to New Orleans and set up strong defenses near the city. His men built walls of logs and dirt on top of wood and cotton bales to hide behind while they fought. The British were foolish enough to attack them there.

| The Battle of New Orleans

The British attacked in January of 1815 with an army of about 10,000 men. Many of their soldiers had fought in Europe, and they knew their jobs well. The Americans, on the other hand, had about 7,000 men from the militia, the army, and others who just volunteered to help (including some pirates). Most of them, however, were frontiersmen and very good shots.

| Reenactment of British soldiers, also called Redcoats because of the uniforms they wore

The British marched straight at the defenses all in a line, wearing their bright red coats, just like at Bunker Hill. The sharp shooting Americans just had to pick a target. The air was quickly filled with smoke from their guns as the British were mowed down like grass. About three hundred British soldiers were killed and more than a thousand wounded. Only about fourteen Americans died. It was the biggest American victory of the war, and it made Andrew Jackson a national hero.

Results. Two important things happened because of the War of 1812. The first was the increase of nationalism in America. The second was the increase of manufacturing in the northeast.

Many Americas thought that we had won the War of 1812. We had fought Britain again and not lost any of our land. Andrew Jackson had beaten some of their finest soldiers (even if it had been after the war was finished). America proved it could stand against even the most powerful nation on earth. The whole

| The 15 star American flag

HISTORY & GEOGRAPHY 503

LIFEPAC TEST

NAME _____

DATE _____

SCORE _____

HISTORY & GEOGRAPHY 503: LIFEPAC TEST

Match these people (each answer, 2 points).

1. _____ Won the Battle of Lake Erie

2. _____ Elected president without any opposition

3. _____ Saved many of the treasures in the White House from being burned

4. _____ Invented the steamboat

5. _____ Won the Battle of Fallen Timbers

6. _____ Built the Erie Canal

7. _____ Explored the land purchased by Jefferson

8. _____ Chosen by the House of Representatives to be president

9. _____ Won the Battle of Tippecanoe

10. _____ Wrote the "Star Spangled Banner"

a. Robert Fulton

b. DeWitt Clinton

c. Mad Anthony Wayne

d. William Henry Harrison

e. Oliver Perry

f. Francis Scott Key

g. James Madison

h. Dolley Madison

i. John Quincy Adams

j. James Monroe

Write *true* or *false* in the blank (each answer, 1 point).

11. _____ The people of the west did not want high tariffs.

12. _____ Andrew Jackson was defeated in the Battle of New Orleans.

13. _____ As part of the Missouri Compromise, Missouri was admitted to the Union as a free state.

14. _____ The War of 1812 helped to increase American manufacturing in the northeast.

15. _____ The Barbary Coast pirates defeated the U.S. Navy in 1801.

Answer this question (5 points).

16. Why did the U.S. go to war with Britain in 1812?

_____

_____

_____

_____

Match these items (each answer, 2 points).

17. _____ Ended the War of 1812

18. _____ Forbade slavery north of the southern border of Missouri in the U.S. territories

19. _____ Political party that so opposed taxes that it did not gather money to prepare for the War of 1812

20. _____ The battle America won after the War of 1812 was finished

21. _____ Andrew Jackson defeated the Creek Indians

22. _____ America warned the Europeans not to take any more colonies in the Americas

23. _____ Explored the land purchased by Jefferson

24. _____ Battle that stopped an invasion of New York

25. _____ Young Congressmen from the south and west that wanted to fight with Britain

26. _____ The "Star Spangled Banner" still flew over this after the battle for Baltimore

27. _____ The way settlers used to reach St. Louis

28. _____ Henry Clay's idea to use tax money to pay for roads and canals; it was not done

29. _____ Land bought from France in 1803 for 3¢ an acre

a. American System
b. Lewis and Clark Expedition
c. War Hawks
d. Louisiana Purchase
e. *U.S.S. Constitution*
f. Treaty of Ghent
g. *U.S.S. Chesapeake*
h. Great Compromiser
i. Tecumseh Confederacy
j. *Adams-Onis Treaty*
k. Missouri Compromise
l. Whigs
m. Democratic Republican
n. New Orleans
o. Plattsburgh Bay
p. Monroe Doctrine
q. Horseshoe Bend
r. Fort McHenry
s. National Road
t. Lancaster Turnpike

HIS 503 LIFEPAC TEST

30. _____ American warship the British had fired upon and taken four sailors before the War of 1812

31. _____ A name given to Henry Clay

32. _____ America's most famous warship in the War of 1812

33. _____ First hard surface toll road in America, in Pennsylvania

34. _____ The U.S. received Florida from Spain

35. _____ Alliance of Native Americans along the Mississippi River

36. _____ Political party founded by Henry Clay and John Quincy Adams when the Democratic-Republican split apart

Complete these sentences (each answer, 3 points).

37. After the War of 1812, Americans were united in a love of their nation called _____ . Later, people from the west, north and south were more interested in the needs of their section, which was called _____ .

38. The _____ was a tax on foreign goods that protected American manufacturers.

39. Jefferson stopped all trade with an _____ to try to force the British and French to respect our ships.

40. People who went to settle the frontier were called _____ .

41. _____ was when British warships stopped American ships and took sailors off them to serve in their navy.

42. The War of 1812 is also called the Second _____ _____ .

43. _____ allowed Americans to trade up and down their rivers after 1807.

44. The _____ Canal was the most successful canal in U.S. history.

45. The _____ political party was founded by Andrew Jackson and still exists today.

nation was proud and happy. They were glad to be Americans. This is called *nationalism*, the love of your own nation. The young nation had survived a tough test and come out united.

A second result of the war came from all the trouble with trade. During the embargo and the war, trade had been almost impossible. Many of the rich merchants of the northeast, therefore, began to build more factories. These could make the goods America could not get from Europe during the war. This started America on the way to becoming the greatest manufacturing nation on earth.

The new factories in the northeast also changed things for the U.S. government. Tariffs had been used only to raise money the government needed before the War of 1812. After the war, they were used to protect American manufacturing.

Tariffs protected American factories by making **foreign** goods more expensive. The cost of the tariff was added onto the price of foreign goods. For example, suppose American hammers sold for 5¢, but the British hammers were 4¢. People naturally bought the British hammers. The American factory would close because no one was buying their hammers. The factory workers would lose their jobs. However, if a 2¢ tariff was put on the British goods, it raised their price to 6¢. People then bought the cheaper American

AMERICAN
Hammers
5¢

BRITISH
Hammers
4¢ 6¢
TARIFF
PRICE

| Tariffs on British goods made people buy more American products.

hammers. The factory owner made money and hired more people to make more hammers. However, this only helped factories. Farmers had to pay 5¢ for their hammers instead of 4¢. Tariffs made all the things they had to buy more expensive. They did not like this.

In places like the south and west, where there were very few factories, tariffs were not popular. However, as more and more factories were built, tariffs got higher and higher. The rich and powerful north wanted more of them, while the south and west wanted less.

Answer these questions.

2.20   What was the name of the treaty that ended the War of 1812?

_____

2.21   Who was the hero of the Battle of New Orleans? _____

2.22   What was the name of the battle where Jackson defeated the Creek Indians?

_____

2.23   Why did the British decide to make peace on good terms?

_____

_____

2.24   Why would Andrew Jackson especially hate the British?

_____

_____

2.25   What two things increased because of the War of 1812?

_____

2.26   How did tariffs help American factories?

_____

_____

2.27   Why was the Battle of New Orleans an unusual victory?

_____

2.28   What part of the country liked tariffs?

a. _____

What parts did not like them?

b. _____

2.29   What was Andrew Jackson's nickname? _____

Review the material in this section to prepare for the Self Test. The Self Test will check your understanding of this section and will review the previous section. Any items you miss on this test will show you what areas you will need to restudy in order to prepare for the unit test.

SELF TEST 2

Match these people (each answer, 2 points).

2.01 _____ Shawnee chief who organized a
Confederacy to stop the American
settlers

2.02 _____ Saved many of the White House
treasures from the British

2.03 _____ Wrote the "Star Spangled Banner"

2.04 _____ President during the War of 1812

2.05 _____ Won the Battle of Plattsburgh Bay

2.06 _____ Won the Battle of Lake Erie

2.07 _____ Led an expedition to explore the
Louisiana Purchase

2.08 _____ Won the Battles of Tippecanoe and Thames River

2.09 _____ Won the Battle of New Orleans

2.010 _____ Sent the navy to attack Tripoli on the Barbary Coast

a. Andrew Jackson

b. William Henry Harrison

c. Francis Scott Key

d. Thomas Macdonough

e. James Madison

f. Thomas Jefferson

g. Tecumseh

h. Lewis and Clark

i. Oliver Perry

j. Dolley Madison

Answer these questions (each answer, 4 points).

2.011 Why was America not ready for the War of 1812?

_____

_____

2.012 Who were the people of Canada who fought so hard against the Americans?

_____

_____

2.013 Why did Thomas Jefferson not believe he could make the Louisiana Purchase and
why did he do it?

_____

_____

2.014   Why did the British finally agree to a fair peace in the War of 1812?

_____

_____

2.015   Why was the Battle of New Orleans so unusual?

_____

_____

2.016   How did a tariff help American factories?

_____

_____

2.017   What did the British do when they took Washington, D.C. in 1814?

_____

_____

2.018   What was impressment?

_____

_____

2.019   What was stopped by the American victory at the Battle of Plattsburgh Bay?

_____

_____

2.020   What was the Louisiana Purchase?

_____

_____

Choose the correct answer from the list below (each answer, 2 points).

nationalism	Treaty of Ghent	*Constitution*	Horseshoe Bend
manufacturing	*Chesapeake*	War Hawks	pioneers
Fallen Timbers	embargo		

2.021 Two results of the War of 1812 were the increase of both

_____ and _____

in America.

2.022 "Mad Anthony" Wayne won the Battle of _____

that subdued the Indians in the Northwest Territory for several years.

2.023 A British ship attacked the *U.S.S.* _____ , killed

several men and took four sailors before the War of 1812.

2.024 The _____ were mostly young Congressmen

from the west and south who thought the U.S. should fight Britain.

2.025 People who moved to the frontier were called _____ .

2.026 The most famous American warship of the War of 1812 was the *U.S.S.*

_____ .

2.027 The _____ said nothing about impressment;

it just ended the War of 1812 and gave both sides back their land.

2.028 Andrew Jackson and the Tennessee militia defeated the Creek Indians at the Battle

of _____ .

2.029 The _____ hurt America by stopping all her trade

without hurting Britain and France the way Thomas Jefferson wanted.

Write *true* or *false* in the blank (each answer, 2 points).

2.030 _____ The War of 1812 was also called the Second War for Independence because we fought to make Britain respect our rights as a nation.

2.031 _____ Many people who moved to the frontier often spent their whole life in a log cabin.

2.032 _____ Thomas Jefferson and the Democratic-Republican Party wanted a weak federal government.

2.033 _____ Andrew Jackson was born into a wealthy family.

2.034 _____ The frontier helped to make Americans freedom loving and strong.

2.035 _____ The British burned Baltimore during the War of 1812.

2.036 _____ The northeast wanted tariffs, but the south did not.

2.037 _____ The American navy did very well in ship to ship battles during the War of 1812.

2.038 _____ Much of New England did not want to go to war with Britain.

Teacher check:

Score _____

Initials _____

Date _____

78
/
98

3. CHANGES AFTER THE WAR

The time after the War of 1812 was a good time for the United States. Everyone was proud of our nation. People wanted to work together, to compromise on problems, and to do things that would unite the nation. The nation was so united that almost everyone even voted for the same political party, the Democratic-Republicans.

However, the good times did not last. Different sections of the country wanted different things from the government. They began to argue against the other sections. The Democratic-Republican Party split apart, too. The north and south began to argue more and more over tariffs and slavery. This section will tell you about these things.

This section also will teach you about how Americans found better ways to move cargo in our nation. New roads, canals, and boats were built to do this. These led to more trade inside the United States which made our people richer.

Objectives

Review these objectives. When you have completed this section, you should be able to:

2. Describe the continuing battles between the United States and the Native Americans.
7. Describe the changes and important events of the years after the War of 1812.
8. Describe the important changes in transportation in America in the early 1800s.

Vocabulary

Study these new words. Learning the meanings of these words is a good study habit and will improve your understanding of this LIFEPAC.

benefit (ben' ə fit). Anything which is for the good of a person or thing; advantage.

prosperous (pros' pər əs). Successful; thriving; doing well; fortunate.

raw materials (rô mə tir' ē əl). A substance in its natural state; any product that comes from mines, farms, forests or the like before it is prepared for use in factories, mills and similar places; coal, coffee beans, iron ore, cotton, and hides are raw materials.

rut (rut). A track made in the ground by wheels.

toll (tōl). A charge for a certain service.

Pronunciation Key: hat, āge, cãre, fär; let, ēqual, tėrm; it, īce; hot, ōpen, ôrder; oil; out; cup, pu̇t, rüle; child; long; thin; /ŦH/ for then; /zh/ for measure; /u/ or /ə/ represents /a/ in about, /e/ in taken, /i/ in pencil, /o/ in lemon, and /u/ in circus.

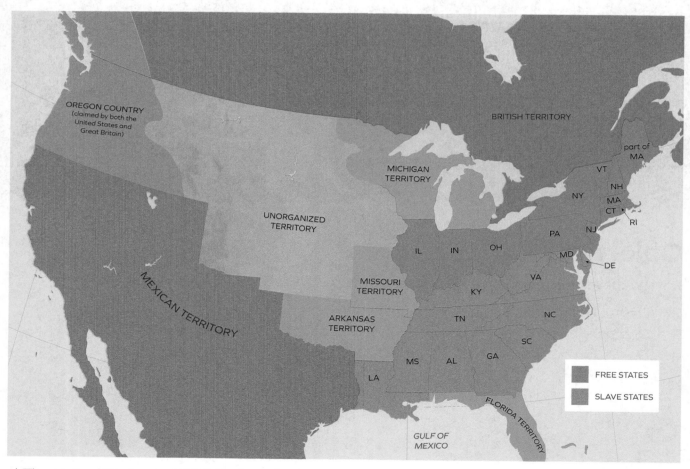

| The United States in 1820 (before the Missouri Compromise)

Good Feelings

The time after the War of 1812 was called a time of "Good Feelings" by the newspapers. America had stood up to Britain and won respect for itself. The country was united. Nationalism was high. The Democratic-Republicans were the party of the whole nation. The Federalist Party was slowly disappearing.

After James Madison retired, the nation chose yet another Democratic-Republican president from Virginia (Jefferson and Madison were both from Virginia, as was Washington). His name was James Monroe, our fifth president. He served two terms as president, beginning in 1817. He was the only candidate for president in 1820. He and George Washington were the only presidents ever to be elected unopposed.

Florida. Florida was the only piece of land east of the Mississippi that was not part of the U.S. after the War of 1812. The American government took part of west Florida from Spain before 1815. That land was added to the states of Louisiana, Mississippi, and Alabama. The U.S. wanted to buy the rest of the territory, but Spain would not sell it.

After the War of 1812, Indians, thieves, and runaway slaves began to attack from Florida where they lived. When they needed money or wanted something, they would attack the American settlers in Georgia or Alabama; then they would run back to Florida. The American army could not follow them into the land of another country. Americans got more and more frustrated by this.

The American government finally decided to send Andrew Jackson into Florida. He was supposed to just punish the Indians and stop them from attacking. However, Jackson had always hated Indians, so he went further. He captured two Spanish outposts and killed some British men who were helping the Indians.

| President James Monroe

The Spanish government realized that the Americans could attack Florida any time they wanted. They decided to go ahead and sell it. Spain and America signed a treaty in 1819 called the *Adams-Onis Treaty*. It gave Florida to the U.S. In exchange, America agreed to give $5 million to pay off some Spanish debts. The treaty also settled the exact boundary between the Louisiana Purchase and the Spanish lands south of it.

American System. Henry Clay of Kentucky had been one of the War Hawks. He was a very good public speaker. He was a leader in the House of Representatives and would be one in the Senate later in his life. He was a Democratic-Republican, but he really believed in a strong federal government. In 1823 he was the Speaker of the House—the head of the House of Representatives.

Clay wanted to make something he called the "American System" to help the whole country. His system was to raise tariffs to protect American factories and use the money to build roads and canals for the farmers. Farmers could use the roads to bring in food and supplies the factories needed. The whole country would **benefit**. The farmers would have a place to sell their crops and the factories a place to sell the things they built. Many people liked this idea.

However, President Monroe was a stubborn believer in Democratic-Republican ideas. He wanted to do only what the Constitution allowed. He did not believe the federal government could use money to build roads or canals inside any one state. Most of the roads had to be built between cities in one state which would connect to roads from another state. Since most of the roads did not cross state lines, Monroe would not sign the laws to build them. The tariffs, however, were passed (became law). That made the south very angry because they had to pay higher prices without getting anything for it.

| Henry Clay

Missouri Compromise. The Founding Fathers had to compromise over slavery in 1787 to write the Constitution. The new leaders had to do it again in 1820. They did this because they did not want to divide the nation. The south insisted on protecting slavery at all costs. It would be many years before the north was ready to fight slavery even when it meant dividing the country.

The north was the fastest growing part of the nation in the early 1800s. Factories were hiring workers and cities were growing quickly. As a result, the north had more votes than the south in the House of Representatives. However, there were 11 slave states and 11 free states in 1820. That meant that the two sides had equal votes in the Senate.

The problem in 1820 was Missouri. It was a territory that wanted to be admitted as a new state. It also had slavery. The northern states were beginning to want to end slavery in the U.S. Many people hoped to do this gradually. The House of Representatives, therefore, said that Missouri could become a state only if it began to end slavery. That caused a major fuss in the south.

The south wanted slavery to grow with the nation. They were afraid of what might happen if there were more free states than slave states. If the free states had more votes in both the House <u>and</u> Senate, it could outlaw slavery. With the two sides equal, the Senate could stop any laws that hurt slavery. (Remember both the Senate and the House must pass any law.) So, the south was determined to have Missouri admitted as a slave state. The northern Congressmen refused to admit it. It was Henry Clay who came up with a compromise.

| Missouri farm

Maine had been a part of Massachusetts since the Revolution. It asked to be admitted as a state, and it had no slaves. As part of the compromise, Missouri and Maine were both admitted. That kept the balance of power in the Senate. There would now be 12 slave states and 12 free states. But, that was only part of the agreement.

Both sides also agreed to draw a line across the Louisiana Purchase. Any new states north of the line would never allow slavery. The line they drew was the southern boundary of Missouri. It was at 36° 30' north latitude. (That is a map line on the globe.) The south was glad to have Missouri as a slave state, while the north was glad that the large northern part of the Louisiana Purchase would never have slavery.

This was a very important compromise called the *Missouri Compromise*. Both sides would keep it for over thirty years. It was important because otherwise the United States might have split apart. The south was not going to lose its slaves, and the north was not yet ready to fight a war to free them. That would come later.

It is also important that Henry Clay came up with this compromise. He believed in a strong United States. He worked hard to solve problems and find compromises. This compromise was one of his most famous, but there would be many more. He became known as the "Great Compromiser." He would play a very important part in finding compromises that kept the United States together until the Civil War (which would happen in 1861).

| The Missouri Compromise

Put an X by the things that are true for each subject.

3.1   Henry Clay

a. _____ He came up with the Missouri Compromise.

b. _____ He was a leader in Congress.

c. _____ He was a poor public speaker.

d. _____ He believed in a weak federal government.

e. _____ He was from New York.

f. _____ He had been against the war with Britain in 1812.

g. _____ He became known as the Great Compromiser.

3.2 American System

a. _____ Tariffs were supposed to protect American manufacturers.

b. _____ The tariffs were not passed.

c. _____ Henry Clay opposed it.

d. _____ It would have built roads and canals for the farmers.

e. _____ James Monroe opposed using federal money inside states.

3.3 Florida

a. _____ It belonged to France at the end of the War of 1812.

b. _____ Indians were using it as a base to raid into the U.S.

c. _____ Andrew Jackson was sent in to conquer the territory.

d. _____ It became part of the U.S. in the *Adams-Onis Treaty*.

e. _____ The U.S. took it without any payment.

f. _____ Jackson's attacks convinced Spain to sell it.

3.4 The Missouri Compromise

a. _____ Maine was admitted as a slave state.

b. _____ A line was drawn across the Louisiana Purchase at 36° 30'.

c. _____ Missouri was admitted as a slave state.

d. _____ Slavery was not allowed north of the line in the Louisiana Purchase.

e. _____ The line was drawn at the norther border of Missouri.

3.5 James Monroe

a. _____ He was a Federalist.

b. _____ He was from Virginia.

c. _____ He was our fifth president.

d. _____ He ran unopposed in 1820.

e. _____ He was president during a time of "Good Feelings."

Not-So-Good Feelings

| Simón Bolívar fought for Colombian Independence.

Monroe Doctrine. During the wars in Europe, Spain had been conquered by France. The Spanish king returned to his throne after the war. However, many of the Spanish colonies in North and South America became independent during this time, while the French ruled in Spain. For example, Mexico became independent in 1821, Argentina in 1816, and Colombia in 1819. These nations usually followed the example of the United States and created republics. The United States wanted to protect these new nations that had followed us in the footsteps of freedom.

After the wars, many of the European kings who had fled were put back on their thrones. These kings did not like democracy in any form. The U.S. was afraid that they might send armies to help Spain regain its colonies. Large armies from Europe in North or South America would be a threat to the United States. President Monroe decided to warn them to stay away.

President Monroe made a public statement that we call the *Monroe Doctrine*. He said that the European countries could not take any more colonies in America. They could keep the ones they still had, like the British and French islands in the West Indies. However, they could not retake those lost by Spain or take any new ones. If they did try to take any colonies here, the United States would react as if they were threatening our land and people. We might even go to war.

The Monroe Doctrine was a very important part of American foreign policy for many, many years. (Foreign policy is the rules our country makes about how it will treat other countries.) The Monroe Doctrine said that the United States would protect the new republics near us. Over the years, many American presidents believed it also meant the U.S. was the boss nation in North and South America. Many things would be done to "protect" our neighbors that were really not very fair. For example, in the future, the U.S. would send its army to collect taxes in some of the small, weak countries of Central America and use the money to pay their debts. The Doctrine was like many things—both good and bad, depending on how it was used.

Sectionalism. The time of Good Feelings ended after 1820. The Missouri Compromise had stopped a major fight between the south and the north. However, both sides were starting to be suspicious of each other. The nationalism of the time of Good Feelings changed to *sectionalism*. This was a feeling that people should love and support their section of the country.

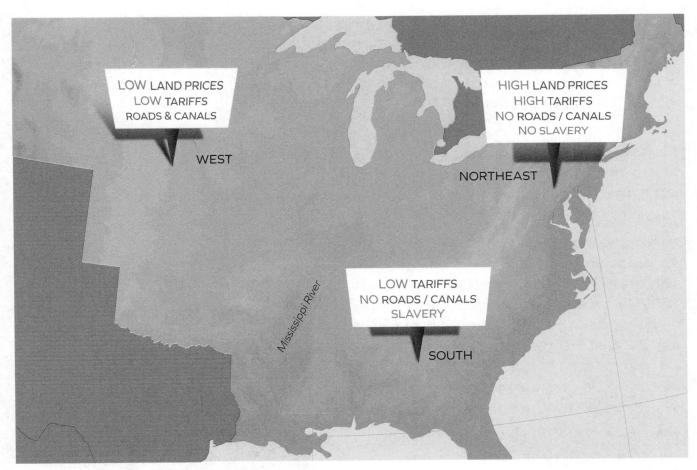

| Regional differences

Each section of the U.S., the north, south, and west, had its own list of what it wanted from the government.

The north (north and east of the Appalachians) wanted high tariffs to protect their factories. They also wanted land in the west (sold by the government) to be expensive. They did not want their factory workers to move west and buy land. They also did not want more states joining the Union that would vote against tariffs. For those same reasons, they did not want the federal government to build roads and canals that would allow the west to trade its crops with the east. That would encourage people to move west. The north also did not want slavery in the new territories.

The south, on the other hand, wanted low tariffs. Tariffs hurt foreign trade and increased prices. The south sold most of its cotton and many of its other crops in Europe. They wanted more, not less, trade with Europe. They also opposed having the federal government build roads and canals in the west. They traded with Europe and saw no need for those things. Most importantly, the south wanted slavery to spread west into the territories. That way there would be more slave-holding states to vote in the Congress.

The west had a third opinion. The west wanted low prices for land. That way the pioneers could afford more land, and more people would move west. The west also wanted roads and canals built by the federal government. They needed these to move their extra crops east to sell and to get store goods they could not make for themselves. They also wanted low tariffs to keep the price of those store goods low.

Even without federal money, roads and canals were built in the west. In time, the west began to build its own factories and cities. Some of the differences between the north and west then went away. However, the differences between the north and the south would get much worse. At first, the two sections argued over the tariff, and later, over slavery. However, it was slavery that would bring the two sides to war.

Democratic-Republicans divide. James Monroe had been the only candidate for president in 1820; however, that was not true in 1824. Four men ran for president that year: Andrew Jackson from Tennessee (hero of New Orleans), Henry Clay of Kentucky, John Quincy Adams of Massachusetts (son of John Adams) and William Crawford of Georgia. They were all Democratic-Republicans, too.

| John Quincy Adams

When the votes were counted, no one had enough to win. The Constitution says that when that happens, the House of Representatives chooses who will be the next president. They choose between the three candidates with the most votes. Henry Clay had the fewest, so he could not become president.

Andrew Jackson had the most votes, so he expected the House to just choose him. However, Henry Clay was the Speaker of the House, and he did not like Jackson at all. He convinced his friends in the House of Representatives to vote for John Quincy Adams, who became our sixth president. Adams immediately gave Henry Clay the job of Secretary of State.

Andrew Jackson was furious. He believed that Adams had bribed Henry Clay with the cabinet job to get the votes he needed to become president. It probably was not true, but it really looked bad. Because of this election, the Democratic-Republican Party split. The followers of Andrew Jackson became the Democratic Party, which is the same party we have today. The followers of Henry Clay and John Quincy Adams became the Whig Party, which would last about thirty years.

Andrew Jackson was determined to become president. He worked hard for the next four years to get ready. He ran again in 1828 against John Quincy Adams and won. Adams was elected to the House of Representatives after that and served his country there until his death.

Put an *S*, *N*, or *W* beside each item to show if it was something the south, north, or west wanted. Some will have more than one letter.

3.6 _____ High tariffs

3.7 _____ Low tariffs

3.8 _____ High prices for land

3.9 _____ Low prices for land

3.10 _____ No slavery in the territories

3.11 _____ Slavery in the territories

3.12 _____ Government money for canals and roads

3.13 _____ No government money for canals and roads

Answer these questions.

3.14 What happened to many of the Spanish colonies in America after the War of 1812?

_____

3.15 What did the Monroe Doctrine say?

_____

_____

_____

3.16 What were the two big issues that the north and south argued about?

_____

3.17 Why did John Quincy Adams become president in 1824 when Andrew Jackson had

more votes? _____

_____

_____

3.18 What were the two new political parties after 1824?

_____

Roads, Steamboats, and Canals

Roads. The roads in America after the Revolution were terrible. Most of them were deeply **rutted** dirt roads. Rain or snow made them impossible to use. That made it difficult for trade inside the country. Farmers needed to take their crops to cities to sell. Factory cities needed food and **raw materials**. They also needed a way to sell their clothes, shoes, tools, and glass to the western farmers. The bad roads also made it difficult to defend the nation. During the War of 1812, the army had a horrible time trying to move supplies around in New York when that state was being invaded.

Many people realized that the country needed good roads with hard surfaces. The federal government usually would not pay for them, however. Some clever businessmen realized they could make money building roads and charging people to use them. They would build a road with a hard surface between a western city and city in the east. Then they would put a row of sharp pikes across both ends. When someone paid the **toll**, the pikes were turned out of the way. That is why toll roads are sometimes called "turnpikes."

The first turnpike was built between Philadelphia and Lancaster in Pennsylvania in the 1790s. It made a lot of money for the men who paid for it. Philadelphia was a port city, so farmers could bring in crops on the road to be shipped to any city on the east coast. All kinds of goods also went out from Philadelphia to be sold to the settlers of western Pennsylvania. The success of the Lancaster Turnpike encouraged men to build more roads like that. Soon, there were turnpikes all over the country.

| Historic stone bridge over the Cumberland River, on the National Road

The federal government did build at least one important road west, beginning in 1811. It was called the National Road or the Cumberland Road. It ran from Cumberland, Maryland to Vandalia, Illinois. Local roads connected to it so that people could travel on a hard surface road all the way from Baltimore, Maryland on the Atlantic Ocean to St. Louis, Missouri on the Mississippi River. That allowed trade from all over the Mississippi River to reach all of the cities on the Atlantic coast.

This was the road used by many of the pioneers who traveled west of the Mississippi River. They would start their journey traveling west on the National Road. Everything they owned would be in a large wagon covered with a canvas top, called a *covered wagon* or

| Covered wagon or "Conestoga wagon"

Conestoga wagon. It was like a camper pulled by oxen, horses, or mules. It carried the family's food, water, supplies to start a farm, clothes, blankets and some personal things.

The National Road made it easy to reach St. Louis. There, the pioneer family would join up with other families, hire a guide and travel west on one of the many trails in a "wagon train," a long line of wagons. They would go to Oregon or the territories in the Louisiana Purchase. Because of the national road, St. Louis became famous as the starting point for many of the pioneers who settled the far west. Today in St. Louis there is a 630-foot tall arch to remind people that the city was the gateway to the west.

Steamboats. Until railroads were built in the middle of the 1800s, boats were still the best way to move large loads of goods or crops. Horses could only pull so much weight. Boats, on the other hand, could carry a lot more and they did not get tired. So, rivers and lakes were the best way to get large loads from one place to another.

On a river, trade was very easy going downstream. Farmers near the Mississippi River could get their crops to a big city downstream quite simply. They would build a large raft called a "flatboat." They would load their crops onto it and float down the river. In New Orleans or St. Louis, they could sell the crop for money. However, then they had to walk, ride a horse, or paddle a canoe back home.

Large loads could be moved down the river, but not up it. Pushing, pulling, or paddling a large boat full of goods up a long river was just too much work. Rivers were one way streets until the invention of the steamboat in 1807.

| A steamboat

The steam engine had been invented in Europe. It used a fire to make steam which turned the wheels of an engine. It was Robert Fulton who found a good way to put one on a boat. He built the first steamboat, the *Clermont*, in 1807. People made fun of it at first, calling it "Fulton's Folly." But no one was laughing when the boat steamed all the way up the Hudson River to Albany! Finally, Americans had a way to move boatloads of cargo <u>up</u> their rivers.

Soon, steamboats were trading all up and down the rivers of America. They were especially important on the huge Mississippi. That river and its tributaries reached all over the center part of the nation. Goods that reached New Orleans could be sent by ocean ships to any of the cities of the east coast or even to Europe or the West Indies. Suddenly, crops and goods could be traded over most of the country. America became more **prosperous** as people made money farming, manufacturing and shipping because of national trade.

Canals. The one big problem with rivers and lakes was that they did not always go by the fastest way. For example, the only water route for goods going from Pittsburgh in western Pennsylvania to Philadelphia (which was about 300 miles away) was to go thousands of miles down the Ohio and Mississippi Rivers to the ocean and back up along the coast.

After the War of 1812, many states began to fix this problem by building canals. Canals could connect rivers and lakes, making faster ways to travel. The most successful canal was the Erie Canal in New York State. That canal connected Lake Erie to the Mohawk River. Because the Mohawk went into the Hudson River, the Erie Canal actually connected the Great Lakes and the Atlantic Ocean!

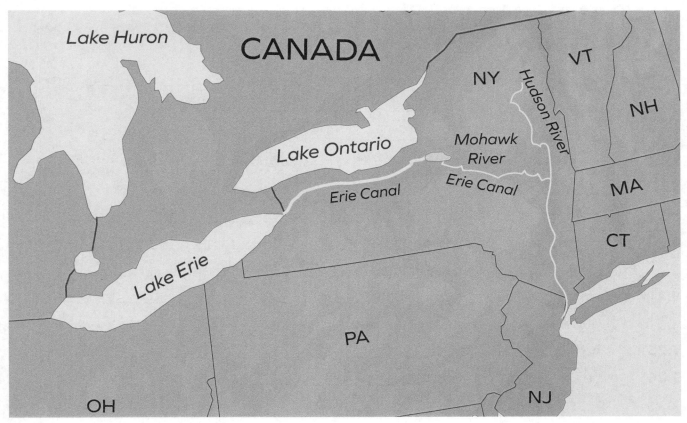

| Map of the Erie Canal

The Erie Canal was the idea of Governor DeWitt Clinton of New York. It was begun in 1817 and finished in 1825. Many people thought it was a silly idea. They called it "Clinton's Ditch." But the Erie Canal allowed farmers all along the Great Lakes to send their crops by a shortcut to New York City. The cost of sending wheat from Buffalo to New York City went from $100 a ton to $5 a ton because of the canal! Other canals were built, connecting the Mississippi River to the Great Lakes, giving all of the Northwest Territory a shortcut to the east coast.

Goods on the Erie Canal moved by barge. The canal barges were big boats made to carry lots of cargo. They were pulled by ropes attached to mules that walked along the side on the "towpath." Some of the boats carried passengers, who sat on top of the boat on fine days. However, the barges had to go under bridges which were just high enough for the top of the boat. When those were coming, the mule driver would yell, "Low bridge! Everybody down!" and the people would have to move off the roof.

The Erie Canal brought a lot of money into New York and New York City. The constant trade helped cities all along the canal. Many other states built canals to connect their rivers and lakes also, but none was ever quite as successful as the Erie Canal.

Complete these sentences.

3.19 The National Road was also called the _____ Road.

3.20 Many of the pioneers who settled in the far west left from

_____ , Missouri.

3.21 Businessmen made money by building hard surface roads called

_____ .

3.22 The inventor of the steamboat was _____ .

3.23 The first steamboat was named the _____ , but

people who made fun of it named it _____ .

3.24 The most successful canal was the _____ in New York,

but people who made fun of it called it _____ .

3.25 The first turnpike was the _____ in Pennsylvania.

3.26 The Erie Canal connected Lake _____ with the

_____ River.

3.27 The man who built the Erie Canal was Governor _____

of New York.

3.28 It was very difficult to trade up a river before the invention of the

_____ .

3.29 By connecting to state roads, travelers on the National Road could go all the way

from _____ , Maryland to _____ , Missouri.

**Before you take this last Self Test, you may want to do one or more of these
self checks.**

1. _____ Read the objectives. See if you can do them.

2. _____ Restudy the material related to any objectives that you cannot do.

3. _____ Use the **SQ3R** study procedure to review the material:
   a. **S**can the sections.
   b. **Q**uestion yourself.
   c. **R**ead to answer your questions.
   d. **R**ecite the answers to yourself.
   e. **R**eview areas you did not understand.

4. _____ Review all vocabulary, activities, and Self Tests, writing a correct answer for
every wrong answer.

SELF TEST 3

Match these people (each answer, 2 points).

3.01 _____ Won the Battles of Tippecanoe and
the Thames River

3.02 _____ Invented the steamboat

3.03 _____ President during the War of 1812

3.04 _____ The Great Compromiser, a War Hawk

3.05 _____ Governor of New York who built a
profitable canal

3.06 _____ Won the Battle of Lake Erie

3.07 _____ President who made the Louisiana
Purchase

3.08 _____ President during the time of Good Feelings, ran unopposed in 1820

3.09 _____ Won the Battle of New Orleans and Horseshoe Bend

3.010 _____ Chosen to be president in 1824 by the House of Representatives, with
Henry Clay's help, even though he did not have the most votes

a.   James Monroe

b.   Henry Clay

c.   Andrew Jackson

d.   Robert Fulton

e.   DeWitt Clinton

f.   Thomas Jefferson

g.   James Madison

h.   Oliver Perry

i.   John Quincy Adams

j.   William Henry Harrison

Complete these sentences (each answer, 3 points).

3.011 The _____ Expedition explored the
Louisiana Purchase bringing back samples and notes from the land.

3.012 The _____ Canal connected the Great Lakes and the
Atlantic Ocean through New York.

3.013 Many pioneers used the _____ Road to reach St. Louis
to begin their trip west of the Mississippi.

3.014 The only political party during the time of Good Feelings was the
_____ created by Thomas Jefferson.

3.015 The _____ Compromise forbade slavery in the Louisiana Purchase north of the southern border of Missouri (36° 30').

3.016 The _____ Doctrine said that European countries could no longer take colonies in the Americas.

3.017 Many of the first hard surface roads in America were _____ built by businessmen who charged people to use them.

3.018 The War of 1812 was also called the Second _____ _____ because America fought Britain again to win respect as a nation.

3.019 Our national anthem is the _____ written about the attack on Fort McHenry during the War of 1812.

3.020 When Missouri joined the United States as a slave state, _____ also joined as a free state.

Choose the correct answer from the list (each answer, 3 points).

American System	Treaty of Ghent	Adams-Onis Treaty	Barbary Coast
Impressment	Plattsburgh Bay	Whig	Democrat
Tecumseh Confederacy		Embargo	

3.021 _____ Political party created by Andrew Jackson, still exists today

3.022 _____ Political party created by Henry Clay and John Quincy Adams when they split with Andrew Jackson

3.023 _____ Alliance of Native Americans along the Mississippi River

3.024 _____ The British took sailors off American ships to serve in their navy

3.025 _____ Gave Florida to the U.S. and set the southern boundary of the Louisiana Purchase with Spain

3.026 _____ Henry Clay's idea to use tariff money to build roads and canals

3.027 _____ Battle on Lake Champlain that stopped the British invading New York in the War of 1812

3.028 _____ Ended the War of 1812 and both sides gave back any land they had captured

3.029 _____ Jefferson sent the U.S. Navy here to attack the pirate nation of Tripoli

3.030 _____ Stopped all trade to try to force France and Britain to respect U.S. ships

Write *true* or *false* in the blank (each answer, 2 points).

3.031 _____ The two big issues the north and south argued about were the tariff and slavery.

3.032 _____ The west wanted low land prices and roads built by the government.

3.033 _____ The federal government usually would not build roads or canals.

3.034 _____ The south wanted slavery in the territories, high tariffs and roads built by the federal government.

3.035 _____ Steamboats made it possible to trade up and down a river.

3.036 _____ America tried to invade Canada in the War of 1812.

3.037 _____ The British burned the important buildings in Washington, D.C. during the War of 1812.

3.038 _____ Canals created short cuts for river and lake travel.

3.039 _____ Sacagawea was an Indian chief who led attacks on Andrew Jackson from Florida.

3.040 _____ The most famous American ship of the War of 1812 was the *U.S.S. Constitution,* also called *Old Ironsides*.

Teacher check: Initials _____   80

Score _____   Date _____   100

Before you take the LIFEPAC Test, you may want to do one or more of these self checks.

1. _____ Read the objectives. See if you can do them.

2. _____ Restudy the material related to any objectives that you cannot do.

3. _____ Use the **SQ3R** study procedure to review the material.

4. _____ Review activities, Self Tests, and LIFEPAC vocabulary words.

5. _____ Restudy areas of weakness indicated by the last Self Test.

NOTES

NOTES

NOTES

NOTES